<u>Minor Poet</u>

"I don't know what I'm saying, but I mean it."
                                                -Watsky

Table Of Contents

29.Love Story
30.You're Right Here
31.Settle Down.

32.Memory
33.Was
34.Was But Again
35.Nebachudnezzar's Nightmare
36.Depths
37.It Snowed
38.Ulcer
39.Matthew
40.Writer's Block, Please.
41.Talking To Myself
42.Popcorn Ceiling
43.Note #19.
44.I Am
45.I Need A Friend

Seventeen

46.Afraid To Love
47.Foreign Words
48.Puppy Love
49.Had I Known
50.Eve
51.I Love You
52.And All The More
53.You
54.Innocence
55.Closeness
56.Stolen Breath
57.Copper's Song
58.Worst Fear
59.A Sparkle In Her Chest
60.Pretty Little Black Dress

61.Self-Appointed Hero
62.To Be Wanted
63.How Vast Is The Emptiness That Surrounds Me

Twenty

<u>Acknowledgements</u>

Robin Williams, N.D. Wilson, Edgar Allen Poe, Watsky, Eminem, Hobo Johnson, Hopsin, Paul Simon, Johnny Cash, Twenty One Pilots, H.P. Lovecraft, Henry Wadsworth Longfellow, Robert Frost, B.O.B, Vsauce, Blink 182, Lupe Fiasco, Ping the Frog, Harambe, Charles Bukowski, Beautiful Eulogy, Aristotle, RadioHead, Friedrich Nietzsche, Paul the Apostle, St. Peter, the Apostle John, The United States Army, Grace Reese Adkins, Marc Webb, Token, Terry A. Davis, Christopher McCandless, Richard "Sky King" Russel, Jack Johnson, Francis A. Schaeffer, G.K. Chesterton, Garth Stein, Jacob Geller, George Lucas, Shrek, Gillian Flynn, Chuck Palahniuk, Kanye West, Albert Einstein, Alan Watts, YouTube, Beetles (the insect, not the band), Black Caviar (the band), Stan Lee, Steve Ditko, Matt Chandler, Bob Ross, John Piper, Frank Abagnale, Christopher Nolan, A.A. Milne, Christopher Robin Milne, Dr. Theodor Suess Geisel, C.S. Lewis, St. Augustine, Bobby Fischer, Ben Affleck, Captain Jack Sparrow, and a special thanks to good coffee.

Connie Mathias (editor), hunter Terrell (wordist), Jesus (the Christ), Chuck Mathias, Jaelynn Muhr, Jason Muhr, Anna Anderson, Anna Muzzarelli, Mikinzie Hoffman, Alyssa Smith, Daycia Kohl, Gabi Rose Young, Ryley Constable, Mike Terrell, Natasha Terrell, Gage Terrell, Aiysha, Cathy Terrell, Larry Orchard, Scot Gilbertson, Max McGee, Rebecca Willet, Micah Burkhalter, Aurora, that one guy I saw drinking at an airport, that one hitchhiker girl I picked up, that old guy I met at McDonald's, and a special thanks to the moon in the daytime.

<u>Foreword</u>

This absurdity sandwich of paper and ink was intended
as an admittedly feeble attempt to roughly catalogue
my human experience in life thus far, with attention
to the way my worldviews changed as I grew. Do not
take it too seriously; I certainly didn't.

I ask that you make no personal judgements of the
author based on your reading. This book contains poems
you dislike. The goal is not to tell you about how I
am; my purpose is to sedate and capture an emotion,
keep it safe, and deliver it as pure and raw as I can
to an audience for digesting.*

Some entries are as old as to have come from my brain
aged eight years, some were written by myself as an
angsty teen, while others were slapped in moments
before publication. Many poems were written with
musical or theatrical intent; sometimes I write to be
heard, not read. And lots of them are super dramatic,
dorky, depressing, or kitsch, let me ask that you bear
it. This book presents the reader with poems in a
certain order, and though it may be tempting to just
flip to the good poems at the back, hopefully reading
them as a complete, cohesive work will be worth it.
This book is an artistic, mostly fictional,
representation of "Real World", and as such should not
be taken literally or used as any sort of how-to guide
for life. The author accepts no liability for any harm
that may befall the reader.

Now, please, point your face at this dead tree and
enjoy.

Eight

<u>Dream Bubble</u>

I dreamed of a bubble
One mile and three inches away;
He was floating along and singing a song—
For he flowed on Sing-a-long Lane.
On his back he carried
Three birds and a berry,
He also carried two pens, a kazoo,
A dog, and paper too.
He was heading towards Mrs K-Mart Sack;
There he would give her rat back.
He borrowed the rat
From Mrs K-Mart sack,
For he had the urge to scratch a rat's back.
If you ask me, he's kind of a whack.
That bubble swore to give it right back,
But there's a problem with that—
Mrs K-Mart Sack lives three toe lengths away
From Far Away Place.
Down the trail he raced
To Far Away Place,
Nearly there
And as fast as a hare—
The bubble flowed as though an Arabian mare.
The bubble reached Mrs K-Mart Sack.
Far Away Place—So that's where she sat!
Thirty-one feet tall
And twenty feet wide;
No one knows what lies inside.
The only way in
Was a hole,
Narrow and thin.
He greeted Mrs K-Mart Sack,
Returned the rat,
And then the dream ended
With the bubble floating back,
Now tell me—
How about that?

Orange

Hi, my name is *orange*!
And I am sad
Because music is all bad.
None of the songs feature me,
And perhaps it's because they can't see
That my rhyme family
Is as big and bright
As my rind and tree.
See, because
This horrid injudiciousness disregards
My porridge storage compartments,
with enormous *door hinges*.
Garages for soup that are guarded
By warnings
Not to break into,
That George
Or Angie ignore,
So that they can forage for,
And gorge
Themselves on all they can eat,
Until more poor journeyers
Join. *Or/and* justice
Is served and the soup eating turds
Are tied up tighter than my Jordans.
Is the problem with orange?
Or in just
Sore, injured poets with *foreign injunctions*
Issued for rhyming *orange*?
The sole use
For this round, cute, little fruit
Isn't just morning juice.
You can't continue
To ignore the rhyming truth.

Sidelines

Watching a soccer game
Can be kind of fun,
Especially when the team
You're cheering for won.

However, watching your own team
Can be kind of tense.
You always want to scream,
"Come on! Where's our defense?"

Everything's in slow motion,
But at the same time high speed.
I feel like a remote
Is just what I need.

As tight as a string
On a guitar, I scream,
"Get another goal,
Or we're gonna get creamed!"

My coach put me in,
But I wasn't doing so fine.
Now I know how they feel
On the sidelines.

<u>America</u>

Born was a nation
Many years ago—
A wonderful place to be,
A home for you and me.
Oh, the place where the free freely roam free!

So many kind faces,
And wide-open spaces,
A government, so strong,
To correct what is wrong,
In the place where the free freely roam free!

One nation under God alone
Such pride in our home—
For the place where the free freely roam free!

All the heroes that died,
The ones who risked their lives,
Twas the fourth of July,
Born the place where the free freely roam free!

<u>Ode To Nipples</u>

Baby you are the one that I know best
And there's something I need to get off my chest.
I need to sing my sorrows away
And you need to hear me say…
Why do I have nipples, what are they even for?
Why do I have nipples, I don't want them anymore.
Why do I have nipples, they are just no fun.
Why do I have nipples,
It's not like I can give milk to anyone!
And people will do the titty twist,
Something that they can't resist.
Before I die, I need to know, what are they for?
I can't do this any longer, am I a freak?
Am I a monster?
Why do guys have nipples?
When it gets cold, they turn rock hard,
Why do guys have nipples? It gets old, it gets hard.
Why do guys have nipples?
Do they do anything at all?
Why do guys have nipples? And why are mine so small?
Do they hold my skin together,
Without them would I fall apart?
Does their hardness tell the weather,
Or are they eyes for my heart?
Why they shrivel is puzzling,
Do these nipples do anything?
God, why did you curse me with these?
They make me want to scream…
WHY DO I HAVE NIPPLES?!
Why do I have nipples, will I ever know?
Why do I have nipples; and why do they haunt me so?
Why do I have nipples; it's a mystery.
Why do I have nipples; the source of my misery.
Why do I have nipples; why do I have nipples?
why... do I... have nipples...?

<u>Hi 5</u>

I guess I always thought I was a fly guy,
Until one day, one kid messed with my brain,
And made me think I might cry.
I raised my hand with a bright smile, and
He said, "Man, nice try!"
I just wanted a simple hi-five.
But this kid went and ruined my life.

'Twas such a disgrace,
That I desired to hi-five him—
In his face.

<u>Eleven</u>

<u>Eleven</u>

<u>School Desk</u>

There is something all you have known
Since year three—
This fun piece
Of furniture, with the gum stuck underneath.
Designed specifically to keep
Students in their seats.

If you need something to write on,
But tables just aren't your thing,
Desks are what you might want,
The education seating king.

Though there is just something
That really bothers me,
It's that you hit the top of your knees,
And there's no room at the bottom for your feet.

If you ever want to keep
A utensil held down,
Then this will wreck your entire week,
Because your pencil rolls around.
Uh-oh, now
You're a brace-faced nerdy freak,
With your TI-83
In the storage compartment underneath.

And your grade average above a B,
Because you learned to stay in your seat,
Five days a week,
For thirteen years of your life.
Never questioning,
Better never ask why,
Because you can rest assured
That the quadratic X and Y
Is the most important thing you will ever learn
In your life.

This chair and table combo

Makes very sure
That your childhood is awful,
That you keep your
Creativity locked away
In a textbook,
With Henry the eighth,
And an x-root.

Raise your hand and ask
To do anything during class.
Just stay quiet so that you pass.
Deep down, you know
The oppressive wounds of education.
You're such a well behaved, learned soul.
And you swear to yourself that
You'll have your fate
When you graduate.
Over and over, saying, "It'll get better,
It will!".
But, for now, you settle down,
Do your work until it hurts,
Turn around,
And
Sit still.

<u>Don't Type</u>

You don't know how to type,
And you look ready
To fight,
Breathing heavy,
You might
Do something stupid
From behind your
Computer tonight.

Log on,
Got 50 likes—
On my selfie,
Looking fly.
Yeah, I'm scrolling fine;
Dank memes are rolling by
And I find
That Harambe died—
Got the world
Wasting time,
Asking God "Why?"
In comments
Late at night.
And grammar died
With the spellcheck hype,
Because your "you're"
Just don't sound right.

#hashtag look at me!
Posting crap in my Twitter feed.
All your followers ain't friends,
A request don't make them,
Because getting featured don't pay rent.
And in the DM's they hating,
Even though they rate ten,
All your subs are fake friends.

And you bet it would be better
If you went to Reddit to lecture her.

She said that it upset her,
Are you getting your feet wetter
As a comment thread editor?

No. So just shut up.
'Cause your memes ain't dank enough,
And trolls got you shaken up,
You hate that gr8 b8 m8,
And you're taking up
This face of caged rage,
That just ain't saying much.

And when you wanna go out to eat with your girl,
She says she don't got no place to eat in the world,
But when your girl just picks, you'll
Be so happy, my rhymes passing—
Wait, slow it down. I just dissed you—I said:
"Your girl's just pixels!"

Confined to a thirteen-inch screen,
Can't be seen
By your browser search history.
This generation of ours is in misery.

We're so clueless,
Don't know where our future is,
Or what we're doing,
But we know what's cool and
Popping, with the memes and the tweets,
Seeing that like button, or something,
Even our dreams are buffering!

Got our whole generation
Messing with the rest
Of the world,
And seven different sects of sex,
Boy or girl.
And the stress of whose six-second video's the best;
When will it end?

There ain't no reset button on life.
Whose left, intact, with their mind?
I look at crap like the dab
And I find, that in fact—
The more crud that's amusing
And the more stuff people doing,
The more that they're losing
Their mind, acting stupid.

And I know I'm a part of it.
God, I got caught up in all of it,
This garbage.
So please help me
To never again take a selfie,
Or scroll through my news feed,
Because all that that is doing is wasting
Time for me, and fading what I find in reality.

So, Internet,
And the users who think they're dope
With Tumblr quotes,
No more days alone,
Locked up at home,
On a pc or smartphone,
Eating out of a garden hose,
No. I propose
That we take down the fricken server
And turn to airplane mode.

<u>Eyes</u>

My left eye sees orange;
My right eye sees blue.
Through the left there is laughter
From sunrise past noon,
But my right eye knows better
Of life and its gloom.
Which eye sees lies;
Which sees the truth?
My left eye is my prize
With all its warm hues.
Then why, why, right eye,
Do I still look through you?

    If the world doesn't look right,
Try using your left eye.

<u>Procrastination</u>

I reckon I'll do it tomorrow.

<u>I Miss The 50s</u>

Someone, please send me back to the '50s,
When folks believed in marriage,
And everybody was pretty,
I don't know I could take one more heartbreak
In 2022.

Send me back to the '60s,
When love was free, there was peace,
And people were hippies,
I can't take one more atrocity
In 2022.

Send me back to the '20s
When people partied sober every day,
And everybody had money,
I can't take one more drunken bum,
In 2022.

Send me back to the '30s
When life was simple, men were modest,
And you could live with no worries,
I can't take one more commercial break
In 2022.

Send me back to the '90s
When kids played outside in real life,
And neighbours spoke kindly,
I can't take one more day
In 2022.

Send me back to the B.C.s
With no rent, no debt,
Back when living was easy,
I can't take one more day
In 2022.

Someone, please send me back to the '50s,
I don't know that I could take one more day In 2022.

<u>I Am From</u>

I am from public education;
From a messed up system.
Xanax flows in our veins, it's intrinsic.
Just sit for a minute
And let me show you around the district.

I am from one hundred eighty days, spending
Eight hours a day, five days a week,
Which sums up to be way too many.
I am from Textbooks and x-roots
And math graphs that seem so petty.
I am from regretting every sentence period
After spending periods
On sentences of pent up stress, intense tests in
Sentenced periods designed to
To drive me delirious;
With failed tests that bear F's
And teachers that take kids way too serious;
With report cards that report stress
And grades that make you furious.

I'm from a school that has to let teachers go
Due to a grand lack of funding,
But can afford to get the football team new buses.
I am from being done with this.

We should fix our obesity problem;
This just ain't right.
I wish someone could afford it.
The district tried to give us crystal light,
But we would just snort it.

I am from number two pencils
And locker room benches.
I am from being too tested
On those school desks that only ever represented
Staff that wants my future headed
In a standardized direction.

<u>#Hashtag</u>

This small box costs a lot.
No, not in dollars, cost;
it is expensive, though.

But its price paid isn't in
dimes, change, fives, Abes,
or credit card swipes made.
Instead, its fine, its sacrifice,
is finally taken
in time... wasted.

Lives fade inside this Myspace of mine that
I've created.
'Cause this world would prefer to see my page,
rather than my face.

And these women didn't feel beautiful
until they saw
those double heart eyes;
fake, typed praise, and likes.
Great! Now you know inside your soul
that life's going the right way.

And when a user validates, you feel it physically,
because you left your phone on vibrate.
As pixels replace silver nitrate,
smiles die behind red-eye corrected selfies
that self-negate
in a designated time frame.

And she can't just think
that she seems really popular.
To believe it, she needs legitimate,
countable followers.

Shout out to all the gossipers.
Users abuse double-edged keyboards;
With lips so quick to spit an acidic derogative

so long as it's on an anonymous comment.

Participate in real life, yet do it bitterly,
so you can use your Twitter feed
to spew some different things
all about your newest spiritual epiphany.

I see a sea of iPhones and emojis;
it's an ocean; like I'm drowning.

Send that "lol" whilst you're frowning.
And it's pointless, 'cause communication is broken.
So she types to him,
"I'm so in love with you."
Yet in her face, she shows no emotion.

I swear I'ma snap if one more person
takes another snap
while I'm trying to hold a conversation.
If you aren't pretty without your puppy ears and nose,
then pose in front of a different congregation.

Just keep swiping right;
your soulmate is out there.
And it's good that they can't smell your profile pic,
because the shower causes condensation.

Just keep things long distance,
so that way you can stay at home.
I'm just trying to connect with her,
but it feels like she's on airplane mode.

Please! I hate that!
Say something, anything.
Look up from your phone
and look me in the face, man.

I'm just trying to start a relationship.
But to her, flirting has been reduced to an eggplant.

Just log on.
There's a whole world out there, so
let's look at it through this small glowing box.

You can roam freely and see Fiji
without any old spice or makeup.
You can meet people,
and even make love,
fight aliens, and show off…

All without touching that doorknob.
All that, and I've left my bedroom door locked.

I can always delete the things that I don't want.
And when I'm with Google, I know that I know lots.
See, I can be beautiful—so long as I got photoshop.

We spend so much time on wifi
that we might idolize our lord, Jobs.
And even begin to see that buffering sign
on our own thoughts.

<u>Five P.M</u>

The walk home at five pm,
Tired and bored and ready for bed;
Just wanna do nothing,
You did nothing all day,
One more day of nothing
Will be okay.

Step over the same crack in the cement
That you've stepped over a million times.
You just gotta make rent;
Is that all there is to life?
And one day
You look up
At the same old grey sky,
And you ask yourself why.

Hanging in until Friday comes,
But Fridays come
Four times a month.
Once a year on the same darn day,
You get a little older,
Go to the same place,
Sit at the same seat,
Ride the same bus,
Eat the same meal,
Number three with nonfat milk.

The same twenty songs come on
The same station,
And at the same darn park
On your annual vacation—
You look up
At the same old grey sky,
And you ask why.
Is this all there is to life?

Stay in school,
Go to work,

Pay your bills,
Invest real good,
Retire early,
And then surely,
Your life will have been worth
Something before you die.

But when you're sitting in your same old chair
At a quarter to nine,
You'll come to find
That there's more to life.

See, people spend so long worrying
About how they're gonna survive,
And they devote and give all their time
To trying to live a good life,
That they forget
To be alive.

<u>Rebel</u>

Obscurity is commonplace
And normality is absurd;
If in sincerity you wish to rebel,
Then you mustn't say a word.

If you want to start a revolution-
Stop complaining
And start at the revelation
That the world doesn't revolve
Around you and your revolting acts
The real resolution is a resolve
To solve the planet's problems,
Start with that.

<u>What Will You Be When You Grow Up?</u>

What will I do in life?
Why do people keep asking this?
They all treat it like—
If I'm not a doctor, eating halibut,
Then I'm all but inadequate.
Who will I be?
No… Who will I be acting as?
I won't confess my profession,
Don't profess what I dress as.
How I make *it* doesn't make *me*,
It ain't even the half of it.
People keep faking,
To blend into the mess of masses,
Just like they were Catholics.
What will I be passing as?
What do I want to be when I grow up?
They all are asking us;
If you insist that I answer, uhh-
I want to be strong.
I want to be kind.
I want to be smart and have a good mind.
I want to be able
To look into somebody's eyes
And see what they really feel inside.
I don't care,
My position, career path, or degree.
A good person is all I want to be.

<u>The Rabbit</u>

Through the grass and past the trees,
Down in valleys and crossing creeks,
Hopping, skipping, galloping it seems,
So the rabbit runs.

Forever away from the fear of defeat,
Towards a destination never to meet,
As aspirations fall past his feet,
So the rabbit runs.

Take a second, yea, take a week;
Stop for a moment, stop running, please!
But he hasn't time even to breathe,
So the rabbit runs.

From pain and death which make men weak;
"Let me rest"—words he shan't speak;
Onwards until the end he meets,
So the rabbit runs.

<u>Slowing Death</u>

How silly it is, the concept of saving a life.
We only ever prolong death.
We're all on borrowed time.
How curious it is,
The desire to add hours
The difference between nine months
And 120 years
Is negligible at best.
Both are but a breath,
Yet still, we strive to slow death.

We invented shoes
And traded blisters for bad backs.
We invented the furnace
And traded freezing for black lung.
We invented preservatives
And traded weevils for sick blood.
We invented plastics
And traded starvation for cancers.
We invented the internet
And traded illiteracy for apathy.

We love to soften, to run, to delay.
But our bodies will decay,
From the dust we came,
And most of us choose to
Crumble back to earth as slowly as we can.
How we love to rage against the dying of the light.
How I love to light another match.
Trying to stave the hunger and cold,
Keep death at bay.
Chasing comfort and control,
But we only ever slow death.
Still, please, give me just one more day.

<u>Lilac Dreams</u>

Like a lilac, lily, rose,
Spreading petals as it grows,
From the ground of a green grass grove,
With trees that reach toward the sky,
Clouds of white,
So blue with hints of maroon, pink and red.
Tiny needles pick up snow, twinkle, glow,
In the night after Light has slept,
Becoming stars on the reflection of a lake,
That shimmers restlessly, yet still.
All is calm, but breathing;
Alive, yet sleeping.

Air is cold, the fire warm,
Embers dim in the lightning storm.
Rolling thunder crackles loud,
Splitting the night with omnipresent sound,
Surrounded now with only the burning sticks near,
Floating ashes and twirls of smoke.
Smell of damp, touch of wet,
Moss and grass make up a bed.
Night approaches, moonlight chases, coyotes howl,
Silence in places.
Crickets chirp and frogs croak,
But the birds are sleeping, tucked up in the cold.

There! The yellow spreads across the sky!
See it now, with thine own eye,
Fire dwindles, but that's alright,
Cold is leaving, replaced by light.
Don your clothes, shiver still;
Blink real slow, as the world's revealed.
There's trail to hike,
Mountains to climb,
Adventure to be had—
Sweet adventure, sublime.

Find a stick, throw a rock,
There's no human in sight,
No phone, no car; just coffee, hot and black,
Only air, pure and raw.
Pure and raw, sound and sight, taste and smell,
Pain that stings so very well,
Light too bright, ground too soft,
Touch too real, much too not.

Light comes in now, to fully dispel the dark,
And your world fades, you're pulled away,
To something stark.
Eyes open slow, in your throat you moan,
Roll over, pull up the covers,
Check your phone,
Detest your slumber.
Put on your socks, shower hot,
Go to school, then nod off.

Revisit life,
When you next dream.
Revisit fake,
When you next awake.
Every day. Every day. Every day.
The next day till the last day.
The last day awaits.

Fifteen

I would have had happiness know me,
Except, behold:
Never before a more beautiful sight I've seen
Than her, standing there, cutting hair,
At the barber-shop, staring through that
Dirty window screen.
I'm wishing, hoping, praying
That she can please just cut my hair today,
Because I can't go another week
Without her smile as I hand her my receipt.
Now sitting in her swivel chair,
Shivering as she runs her hands
Through my unworthy hair.

Hunter, do, say anything;
Compliment her,
Undo your pocket zipper,
Pull out your wallet,
Tip her;
But instead, I just sit there,
Mesmerised. I define love
By the way I am touched
With those clippers.

She's mystifying
With her misting;
I'm free
From the restraints of her barber's blanket,
Yet held captive by her vacantness,
And the pain the space makes;
She left blank in my chest.

Then I have to get up and leave;
Wait, and count down days
'Till next week,
When I can see her again.

<u>A Thing</u>

I have seen a thing so pretty,
A being that is so serene
That in just being, she is
Pretty pristine.
She makes me think,
Maybe I'd be better if I could think
Straight;
Pretty please let me be.
Great,
She's pricked my peace with pins
So sweet;
Such a tender ping of her
Presence missing is a sting
That I wish would cease.

I have seen a thing.
A pretty thing that
Will test my ability to present myself
Presentably, because I'm really just
Drifting; she's killing me.
Please, I may be distressing and need a
Princess to come rescue me.
She's insistent upon arresting my
Attention with eyes of a crystal creek.
And above the rest, she
Makes me restless; I possess an incessant
Need to love everything that
She is or was or represents.

I have seen a thing,
So pretty,
And so sweet,
That I simply cannot be,
So long as I believe that a thing so pretty
Just may be being; somewhere, out there,
Without me.

<u>Something In Her Eyes</u>

There were a few times
When I thought it would be alright.
We'd go our separate ways,
"Friends forever" will end one of these days.

But then you had to go and
Look back at me.
Wet in the rain;
Hair in your face,
And I could have sworn, I
Saw something in your eyes.

I would have been alright,
If you just kept walking that night,
But you had to go and smile,
And there was just something in your eyes.

It's like we had a conversation
And we both knew
Our lives had changed then.
We thought that we were just friends,
Until I
Noticed something in your eyes.

It gave you away,
And uncovered me;
Nothing would be the same.
It was just a smile, right?
But, there was something in your eyes.

Should Have Stayed Up

I don't know what happened exactly…
But I remember how it felt.
And it's like you could have just asked me
To stay up, just a little hint would have helped.
I don't know why I keep defending
My loneliness above all else.
I was so afraid of a good thing ending,
That I terminated it myself.

I should have stayed up with you all night.
Our heads out the windows, wind was in our hair,
And we felt like we could fly.
I could see just you and me, in the back seat.
Couldn't care who did the driving,
But I seemed
To recall you turning and smiling
At me. Something that I said,
For now, I'm free, but it's fleeting,
Because I went home
And my head hit the pillow on my bed.
And then you all probably did the same…
But we should have kept on going.
There's a creek I used to know and
We could have gone on floating,
Or stolen someone's boat,
Then taken a road trip
To wherever the wind was blowing.
I should have stayed up with you all night,
Who says good things have to end?
I was scared that I might
Have said something that I meant,
But I should have stayed up.
I should have stayed.

<u>Tell You Again</u>

Ink, dripping from the tip of my pen,
Resisting the urge to give up again.
I'm searching for words
That I've already said.
Don't know how to express
What you've already read.
How much I love you,
I'd love to
Tell you again.

Have You Ever?

Let me ask you something;
Have you ever asked someone
That you actually loved
If they loved you back?
And had them say nothing?

Have you ever felt like you had no one,
Because you couldn't have *the* one?

Have you ever gotten high
Off a song you never thought
You liked? But then it was that one song that
Played that one time you first met,
And you spent days amazed
At your physically hurt chest.
It was the worst pain you've ever felt,
Yet it hurt the best.

Worse yet—
Your heart literally physically skips a beat
When you breathe the same air,
But, wait, because she will
Never, ever, irrelevant
Of your vain prayers,
Feel the same way about you.

God, please numb this pain,
But she still has got that same
Blank stare, not again!

Nothing has ever hurt more, in fact,
Than that time when you said
You wanted to be more
Than just friends,

And saw her gorgeous eyes stare back,
With absolutely
No love in them.

<u>Love Story</u>

Reliving every second
And iterating every sentence;
I'm ruminating in shame,
Because I haven't your explicit
Consent to obsess... yet.
Reminiscing in vain; lost and falling apart,
Hunting to catch a breath,
I'm sitting in the dark, hyperventilating
Your name into some sweatshirt that you had left.
Please let it end.
Or can I even ask that?
Because you haven't really ever let it begin.
I attempt to extract compassion out of
Every word that leaves your lips,
Magnifying and reflecting back
My own emotions into this.

I reason with myself at night:
You must love me;
How could you not?
And it never leaves my sight,
The thought
That maybe my dream was right
And when you said we were just friends,
It was not.
I know I come off needy,
Creepy, infatuated,
Or even mad.
I'm sorry; I'm not meaning
To, it's just, it hurts so freaking bad.

I hope you know I love you.
I wish you'd comprehend
My estimation of you,
For I assessed my assortment
Of resources and dismasted
Everything above you.
Because

As for me,
You were enough.
Can't you see-
How, for your love,
I'll gladly travel to hell and back.
I've madly ambled,
You've had me in shambles,
How badly I had to
Tell you that.
I'm not here to make you reciprocate
But from fear lately, I'll stipulate
That you've just been hiding your feelings;
Don't sell me that.

Is it better to have known and to have lost?
Is it better to have had and now have not?
Once I knew an answer with optimism,
But I have forgot.

What did I do to deserve this?
I used to think you were
Almost too perfect,
But now you don't seem to think
I'm even worth it.
I'm not gonna lie, it's hurting,
'Cause I been thinking about the time
You fell asleep in the back of my Buick.
We drove all night,
And it's like there was love and I knew it.

Isn't it crazy? That two people can go in
A matter of days, from eyes full of love,
To a bad type of hate.
I'm leaving tomorrow,
And I'll probably never see you again.
I'll never know why,
I'll always wonder what I did.

<u>You're Right Here</u>

I think of all the nevers as I cry.
Nothing hurts me more than your sad smile.
I miss you more and more as time goes by;
I've missed you for most this year,
And you're right here.

You'll always make me love you,
Even when you don't try.
I tell you, for your sake,
Nothing of the kind.
And you're right here.

In our dreams, we'll be together,
And all will be fine,
Tomorrow we still will,
But it won't be right,
Because you're the ocean,
And I am the dry.
When this all is over,
I can say that I tried,
But I'm the end of this one,
And you'll be just fine.
When the tomb is sealed,
But you haven't died,
Rejoice my child,
Because it's dark inside.

When you ask me why I'm crying,
Nothing hurts me more
Than your sad smile.
And all this time,
Your train was never coming,
Your ticket is expired.
I might have fibbed a little,
But hope's the real liar,
Because you're right here.

<u>Settle Down.</u>

Their words:
        "Settle down."
But I've yet to find a way to make the
Numbness go away,
Except to do something wrong.
I always did have poor balance.

        Perhaps I had gotten out of hand.
She said she loved me,
With her eyes,
But it was with my lips that I said it back.
Her words:
        "Settle down."

Stay, no more can I withstand a lack of company;
Always, always saying all I want is nothing more
Than to meet a girl and marry her—

        And finally
Settle down.

<u>Memory</u>

Once in an important life I led,
To me, many sacred secrets were made known.
And a frequent important line I read,
Knowledge to keep for me to own.

But, alas! Futile as is life,
Life's brutal blow is struck.
For the things I have known in write,
In my mind, have become unstuck.
If I could remember
I might be alright,
Instead, I curse my luck above,
For I might remember what I lost,
But I have forgotten
What it was.

<u>Was</u>

There is a thing so fleeting,
It leaves before its want is known,
Yet men come from near and far,
To try to bring it home.

Tell me, wise men,
Tell me, kings,
What be it that I seek?

I had myself this thing,
But once in a dream.
And now this thing I held so dear;
How, I loathe, can it be?
Because this thing,
I do not now know.
For it has drawn itself from me.

<u>Was But Again</u>

I once have dreamed a dream,
So sweet was it to me,
Yet I know not now what it was,
For this dream is gone from me.

<u>Nebachudnezzar's Nightmare</u>

There is something terrible on the tip of my tongue.
Sleep has left me for some unknown horror
That I have tasted in dreams.
Some awful truth I think I once knew;
Haunting my thoughts—
A shadow on the edge of my view.
All-consuming, the nagging of a memory,
That, while not present, is not absent,
Partially absconded.
Its ghost remains. The stench of its ashes
Controls my physical reactions:
Heart beats faster;
Sucking on as little of the damp air as is possible,
Spitting it out as soon as it hits my throat,
Empty lungs.
Something terrible lurks on the tip of my tongue.
A wriggling parasite I can feel, full well,
Its presence. But search and squeeze as I may,
I am eluded and my grasp is weak.
Something terrible,
And thin, and slippery. I cannot see it,
I do not know it,
But when I awaken to my scream, wet with sweat—
It is clear to me that this terrible
Thing has visited me,
Once again in my dreams.
Something… I think.

<u>Depths</u>

The depths do beckon.
From the chasm echoes his name.
Caves whisper to him;
He is pulled down so very naturally by gravity.
Down. Down. Down. Down.
His feet may be planted on some surface,
But the density of the depths that stretch below
Will not keep him up, nor support his weight.
Give him a harness and some rope, if you will.
Give him a shovel, or a drill.
Give him a flashlight to push against the black.
Give him a map, in case he tries to climb back.
You exist at such great heights;
Ignore that fact.
You can cover the abyss with pavement,
Or even carpet it, if you wish-
That you might not seem to be floating,
So you won't feel your fear of heights.
For him——the ground may well be glass,
And the grass as the top of the tower,
There's still so far to fall.
So much farther down the tunnels do stretch.
Is there an end,
Or will we dig forever?
Water trickles and rivers flow somewhere,
Ice sings hauntingly as it sinks,
The pressure of the depths above are crushing,
And the weight immense.
Air is an illusion;
You exist in such a thin sliver,
Only ever occupying one floor of a tower.
On what, if at all, does the tower rest?
There cannot be a bottom.
He must descend,
Descend.
The depths do beckon.

<u>It Snowed</u>

It's snowing.
I think the planet is spiralling
Down out of control again,
That floating has ceased, and
We've begun the free-fall descent
Into the endlessness.
Sun now forgotten, lost, we spend forever
Spinning. Spinning as our little blue rock drops
And drops
Into the dark, dense, cold.

<u>Ulcer</u>

Tell him to ignore it,
The stress, but instead,
He just writes off steam.
Try to keep
His wife happy,
His life half-decent,
But the sky's blackening,
And he's right past being
In piles of pieces,
That's why he likes that drink.

And he knows his
Cirrhosis will go till
He's comatose.
These *ulcers*
Are an amazing thing.
Crazy, how ironic,
That through all this stuff,
She still finds a way
To give his *stomach*
Some *butterflies*,
But these ones must have
Razor wings.

<u>Matthew</u>

The bar is closing, and you have to
Go home and just relax, dude.
It's so past your curfew,
And that dude is so passed out.

You stagger down the street,
Past a kid holding a hat to
Collect penny donations for some fast food.
Get home and collapse, shoot.

You still got a bottle, but it's broken.
So you grab a Bible
And flip it open to Matthew.

"God, I've been hoping to ask you,
If you could pull me sort of on track soon.

I've tried to stop
Tearing my life apart,
But historically I've made
My poor old mama cry a lot.

I'm to the point where I'm not too sure
Anymore whether I try too hard,
Or don't try at all. I'm tired, but it's cold,
And I kinda don't wanna go one more

Step. I'm on the edge, but I
Bet I can catch my Breath.
They tell me I got to stop,
I don't wanna, they don't get

That I haven't found the
Bottom of my bottle

Yet."

<u>Writer's Block, Please.</u>

Please, God, give me some writer's block.
Some relief from these
Rhymes I write inside my thoughts,
And to myself I talk
As I pray for the words to stop,
Sometimes I believe they are coming to an end,
I pretend, but I know they're not.

Some see it as poetry;
I see it as a disease, see,
It's killing me.
Making it so I can't breathe.
Walking, stumbling, pacing,
Muttering to nobody but me.

All these emotions, all these words, pent up.
You don't know what it's like
To wake up in the middle of the night
And have to write that one line that you dreamt of.

The words are coming even now,
Faster than I can write them down.
I get off track, all over the place,
And I write to cope because that's the only way
That I know how.

Please just a little relief.
Just a little sleep.
Trying to keep
My sanity,
I'll gladly
Have
Just a little piece
Of
Writers
Block,
Please.

<u>Talking To Myself</u>

        One day,
You came out into the world,
Into the bright-white, wide-open blue;
Something that you didn't choose to do,
But you did, and as you did you grew,
And as you grew you never knew
What it would take to stay true,
And the things that you'd have to do
Just to continue to be you.

        See, you didn't ask to be placed on this planet;
That's an accident; you never planned it,
And, man, you'd try to take so you could have, and
You'd stay awake trying to grasp at anything,
Thinking any next breath might be the last,
But Life came up on you too fast;
Took your breath away
And never gave it back.

        You never would have signed up for life
Had you known—
What it felt like to feel so alone.
At home on a Friday night;
Keep looking at the phone,
And then look back and ask yourself,
"What are you still looking for?"

        Tell yourself that it'll be okay.
Even if they never love you,
You'll get through the day;
Waiting, sit and pray
That you are not just insane,
And that the voices talking in your brain
Are just a silly game the devils like to play.
Pray on you,
Making you believe
That you still have sanity left to save.
Try to be brave,

But it already started, it's too late.

       Who are you talking to?
The ardent listeners aren't awake.
Darn it, have you been doing this all day?
The conversation had seemed okay, even heaven-sent.
An ear for you to bore just for the heck of it.
Pour out a little more
Of that pent up stuff that was irrelevant;
Vent.
Until you realized that you were on the speaking
And receiving end of it.

       Please stop.
Please stop.
Please stop.
You just talk,

       Because the voices are getting louder.
Going off so loud it hurts,
And some of them are opting to get out,
It's only getting worse;
Lost, and it seems so absurd,
But your thoughts that you
Thought were just your thoughts
Are somehow now coming out as words.
Oh, how the lines are blurred.
It seems to me that dreams are reality
And that the screams of fantasy
Are actually just a curse.
Now there is no rescue,
Waiting for the hearse.

       There's nothing left to do.
Muttering under your breath to the death of you,
And they all get worried,
Some laugh, mocking, scoffing,
And you yell,
"Leave me alone, can't you tell I'm talking?"
Rocking back and forth,

In the dark on the floor.
You gave up long ago trying to make the voices stop,
You did before, but no more,
Now when you're bored
You just talk, you just talk, you just talk.

        You fought an awful lot
With the talking voices in your head
Oh how you used to, you forgot.
But now it seems your choices are all dead.
Out of options,
So now you got to get along.
Doesn't seem so wrong.
So you just talk.

        It's kind of fun by yourself.
I don't need or even want someone else,
Maybe the voices are mean to you
But they're right, too.
Talk.
Talk because you lost the option to choose.
Talk because it's what we must do.
Talk because you're the only one that will
Listen to you.
Talk.

        You tell yourself you'll quit in the morning,
Swearing, "I will."
But the words aren't working,
World's turning, whirling;
Took too much NyQuil.
So, you just lie still.
Still,
Still muttering.
Still wondering.
What else will life kill?

        Medication, mind vacation, meditation,
Therapists, operations,
But you still got this obligation

To tell other people how you feel,
But that's not real,
Because you're the only person who still gets it
And the only one who ever will,
But the other people still insist,
And you can't resist,
After all, we have some time to kill.
It won't take long though.
So you go home, write a song,
And they thought all along
That you were talking to them,
They were wrong.

        I'm okay, no
You're not.
I gotta get out.
You got to stop right now.
I can't stop; it's too loud.
You want to stop, but
I don't know how.
You can't turn this around.
Am I thinking, or are
You speaking?
We want to scream and shout.

        No, they don't get us; do they?
But that's okay because it's a new day,
And we'll have plenty of time alone,
After I put down this microphone
In the end, and to defend;
I nod and smile, for a while, every now and then,
To make people think
That We're talking
To them.

<u>Popcorn Ceiling</u>

Yeah, I know that. Tell my adrenal glands. Mind over
matter. I exist, I exist, I exist.

The popcorn ceiling that hangs over my bed is
memorised. My troubled mind has read and could
redescribe every line. Every hill, valley, and
scratch. Every berm burned into my cornea for the day
when I regurgitate in burning hate the popcorn ceiling
that hangs above my bed. In the dark. In my head. The
popcorn ceiling that hangs above my bed.

Why am I so weird? I'll be OK, everything will be OK.
I exist. Even when I'm not asleep. I exist.

<u>Note #19.</u>

Fear in my chest,
Tremble in my breath,
The monsters are not,
Underneath our beds,
They are inside us.

Breathing to death,
There is nothing left,
The ghouls we forgot,
Are inside our heads,
Our mind is our closet.

<u>I Am</u>

I am a bird with a broken wing,
Whom people admire for being free,
But only I know I can't fly.
I wonder what I'm meant for;
I wonder how soon I'll die;
I wonder if anyone will mourn; will anyone cry?

I see clouds from only the bottom side
And wonder what it is on the top that they hide.
I am a bird with a broken wing;
They like to hear me sing,
But only I know I can't fly. From the outside
I look alright, but I'll never fly.

I am a bird with a broken wing,
Whom people admire for being free.
And I've never quite known why, but I know,
I know, that I'll never fly.

<u>I Need A Friend</u>

Need a Friend.
I desperately
Need a friend.
I'm beginning to have that same feeling
Of manic panic that's been stealing
All of my freedom. I once defeated
These demons, but I guess they just really
They needed a sequel.
I was just chilling,
Walking down the hallway,
When I started to count all the caulkings;
It was my fault, I started the process
Of wondering about wandering out
Of monotony, stop it, please.
I need to tell someone these things,
I had nothing to say today,
There might be people who'd understand,
But they're very far away
And we don't talk anymore anyway.
A psychiatrist will gut my
College fund
For a few words,
How absurd,
That I'm so desperate just to talk.
I'm hunting for an ear,
Whispering to holes in the wall,
But no one ever hears.

Seventeen

I swear she's gonna kill me.
I don't know what's going on.
I just wanna know what's really
Moulding all my songs.

I swear, she kills me.
Her long blonde hair
Is too real, please,
Someone pick me up,
Because I'm really
Falling for this chick,
And what gets me,
Is that I think maybe she's into me.

I remember being
So lonely and so sad.
And now there's a girl that's real,
And it still
Hurts so very bad.
I cannot eat,
I cannot sleep,
For the dreams I know I'll have.
I think she might love me,
And I'm afraid that I may
Love her back.

<u>Foreign Words</u>

She tells me she loves me,
And those are foreign words.
She tells me she loves me,
And I want so much more it hurts.
Someone come find me,
I'm miles lost in her eyes;
Someone come lie to me,
Say this will all be alright.
Because I'm dying, and yet,
I've never felt more alive.

<u>Puppy Love</u>

Oh my gosh; she gets me.
Got me up in paws, like a dachshund,
Puppy love as if I was 16.
I close my eyes and I'm picturing
Her as a wife; we have children,
And it's bliss because when she's with me—
I get this feeling like the rest of the world
Can just forget me.
This girl is so pretty,
And she loves me freely
Like we was living in the '60s.
No more sitting, sickly wishing
That any girl would just get with me.
Instead, I'm spinning
About how we will be a "we"
'Till we're plenty and well into our 50's.
And past, because, man!
Stick me, Cupid,
I'm in too deep—I'm feeling stupid;
Is this too good to be true?
I feel like stealing glue,
Hoping I can stick to you,
And I'm just trying to play it really cool.
Because she gets me, ooh!
She gets me.

<u>Had I Known</u>

Had I known,
If only;
Had I known a golden fountain flowed
From the top of her head
To the small of her back and wrapped
Around two dear earlobes;
Had I known a single twinkle gleamed
And shone,
In gems of eyes, like precious stones,
And lips so fine that when they spoke
Dripped words of honey, running
Down her neck to glisten on her slender
Collar bone;
And whenst betwixt a kiss is blown
Trees will shiver and winds will moan.
Had I known;
Had I known a heart so deep
Lay just beneath a fair as peach skin tone;
Had I known how I was actually so alone,

I would have loved, I would have held,
From day one, from a prison cell,
Or from a throne;
Had I known, the way she felt,
The way she'd grow,
It is her I would have chosen;
Had I only known.

<u>Eve</u>

If God gave
A blank template,
With which
To create Eve from clay and a rib,
Any deviation from the distinct way that she is
Would be a sin,
For she is perfection,
In all it's essence
And her name retains
A faint resemblance
To sun after a rainy day;
How pretty a sound: "Apricity",
A noun, yea it is
An adjective,
Descriptive in the sense
That she, and her, and everything she is
Leaves me literally breathless.

<u>I Love You</u>

I can't tell you how much I love you because I would
love you more than that by the end of the sentence.

<u>And All The More</u>

I love you when I'm with you,
And all the more when I'm not;
I've loved you as I've kissed you,
And all the more as we fought;
Say you'll let me love you,
And, my dear, I'll never stop.

<u>You</u>

Okay. What's happening?
Like, wow. You actually have me
In shambles. I mean, I'm happy,
But sometimes I happen to act a tad madly.
I'm sorry. I have feelings
That translate into actions, that's not a bad thing,
It's just that I'm not passive.
I'm still ambling,
Attempting to catch up with my gut,
The butterflies have up and taken off;
Ironic that these monarchs rule my heart,
And my thoughts. You are increasingly
The only thing that I ever want. Ever.
Oof, that's a lot. I want you,
And I don't want this wanting to stop.
This is beautiful, but it's scary, it scares me,
Because the very things that I hold dear,
To me, could become a thing I have lost.
You are my very being, unceasingly,
My lung's reason for breathing, my mind's
Reason for thinking, my heart's
Reason for beating. And if ever you must
Leave me, my dear, I fear that my heart
May stop. That's why I'm afraid. Because
I love you more every day, but tomorrow's
Not a promise.

<u>Innocence</u>

I want to protect her,
But I'm afraid I've already failed.
I want her forever,
But that ship may have already sailed.
I want to keep her innocent,
I hope she knows she's golden,
Yet, I fear that when we met,
Her innocence was already broken.
I tell myself
I need someone else,
But her
My heart has chosen.

<u>Closeness</u>

I have lost myself.
No longer am I capable of asking questions
          a snake might.
Such selfish questions like
"What will I be, where will I go, what will I do?"

Now my heart is filled with us.
My organs are crushed by love-pumped blood
And the pressing must of being more filled with us.

I need to be closer,
I'll squeeze you and hold you
And curse our flesh and bones for preventing us
From touching souls.

Hold. Hold. Take your hand, press your shoulders,
          squish your ribs.
To feel your heartbeat, breathe your breath,
          taste your kiss.
Give me closeness.

Promise me forever,
          Or at least until the dawn.
Have me, be mine,
          Just please hold on.

<u>Stolen Breath</u>

The way you make me feel
Is too impossibly real;
You take my breath away
And I'm scared,
Because of so many what ifs,
But now, I think,
There's something I finally get—
It's that, yes, you take my breath away,
But that's okay, because, to me,
You're more important than oxygen.
You take my breath away,
And I gasp,
You took my breath away,
Left me choking, and I'm hoping
That you never have to give it back.

<u>Copper's Song</u>

I wouldn't have known,
Even if you told me.
The woods are my throne
And the clouds are what hold me.

If I could fly, I'd fall with the snow,
And reflect lights in the street,
At night, as cars go by,
In the rain; headlights chasing me.

But I never went there.
I'm too afraid I'd say what I mean,
And it's raining, it's falling,
But I'm only wet at my feet.

So come fly away with me.
I'll take us up and to any anywhere
Because In the sky I'll be free.
There's ground down there, isn't there?

I'm trying to fly,
Please, let me go higher,
I just wanna fly,
Just wanna be free,
So why don't you take my hand,
And come fly with me.

<u>Worst Fear</u>

Her eyes were cold
On the outside,
Because she was never
Loved as a child,
But her mind was
Numb to the world.
She was a lonely kind of a girl.
She saw right through me,
And she said to me:

"I see your pain crystal clear,
And the monsters that still lurk near.
I don't wanna work here
I know it still hurts, dear.
Baby, what's your worst fear?"

"Not being alone someday;
Not dying by myself.
Everyone's going the wrong way,
Looking down at the higher shelf.
Everyone that's with me,
Through my friends and dead-end job;
My worst fear is, and always will be:
That I've been alone all along."

Life's a job, that's clear.
And I don't wanna work here,
It will always hurt, dear,
Just get through this cursed year,
Avoid the monsters that all lurk near,
I can make them disappear.
Baby, what's your worst fear?
What's your worst fear?

<u>A Sparkle In Her Chest</u>

She has a sparkle in her chest;
God put it there when she wasn't paying attention.

I see it glisten in the dew of her breath,
Before the morning sun's ascension.

She has a warmth in her heart
That sharp rains cannot touch.

She has a candle in her stomach,
And love, love, in as much—

As the earth tumbles round through the black,
Her tiny soul still will glow,
And her God will smile back.

<u>Pretty Little Black Dress</u>

I love that pretty little black dress she wears,
Best thing I've ever seen.
I love that pretty little black dress she wears,
The girl of my dreams.

My momma asked me,
What's the best thing I've ever seen,
Momma, it's that pretty black dress,
On the girl of my dreams.

That little black dress said she loved me,
I held that fabric tight,
And sometimes that dress would need,
My comfort when she cried.

I love that pretty little black dress she wears,
Best thing I've ever seen,
I love that pretty black dress on,
The girl in my dreams.

My momma asked me, "Son,
What's the worst thing you've ever seen?".
And I couldn't look my ma' in the eye,
Because, the truth, sometimes it stings.

Let me tell you, mom,
The worst thing that I've known-
That pretty little black dress I love,
On his bedroom floor.

I loved that pretty little black dress she wears,
All cuddled in his arms.
That pretty little black dress of hers,
Left a pretty little black scar.

<u>Self-Appointed Hero</u>

Can't you see my shining armour?
Or the cross etched upon my shield?
It's my duty to let nothing harm her-
I'm her guardian, to see her healed.

Didn't you know it's on my shoulders?
To serve and protect the maiden fair?
I swore an oath to love and hold her;
I promised I would always be there.

Has no one told you I'm supposed to save her?
Haven't you heard of my noble quest?
Just as well. Perhaps if I were only braver
I'd not return alone, nor fail the test.

The tallest towers I scale without hair,
To find dark dungeons with unlocked doors.
Bedrooms thick with drugs in the air,
Hallways with laundry-littered floors...

And the look I get is always the same,
Yet still, I ride, towards the dame in distress,
And still, contented princesses remain—
Seeming ever so dragon-esque.

<u>To Be Wanted</u>

Every time a pretty girl bats her pretty eyes at me,
I drop everything happening in my pitiful
Life that week
And try so very hard to be all the things
She tells me that she likes in me.

OK.

It feels really great to be liked.
I mean, there ain't nothing quite
Like lying in a twin-sized bed
In your parent's basement,
And dreaming of a day when
You never fall asleep alone again.

Man! Nothing beats an empty studio apartment
Around dinnertime. Microwave some frozen food
And wonder what fun it must be to cook for two.

I'm really pretty in love with the idea
Of someone being in love with me;
I just want to be wanted.
I dream to be the object of another's dreams.

Woah!

It's kind of really nice being liked!
When someone says that they like me,
The poems that I write get much happier and I
Lie awake, hope—hope—
Hoping so very hopefully.

And, oh. It really sucks
When they change their mind;
That's a jolt of cold reality.
I'll stop trying to find
A different mattress to buy—
Twin-sized suits me quite perfectly!

How Vast Is The Emptiness That Surrounds Me

Act I

Ocean,
Vast, open sea.
Full of promise,
Promising me,
Promising you.
I always knew.
Hope is a liar.
Too good isn't true.
Prove me wrong,
You will never again
Let me down,
Lead me on,
Because I've come to know
And expect
What makes sense.
I bet we drown.
Please.
I just want to sleep,
But I'm afraid I may dream,
And when I dream, as much
As I wish I'd wake up
And seize that goal I'm
Seeing, as much
As I wish I'd wake up
Screaming, I just wake up believing.
And I hold on, clinging.
My belief doesn't leave until the evening,
When the sun sets and I'm left,
With nothing but an empty chest,
On my deserted island,
Watching crew, family, and best
Friends sail off in my ship.

Act II

Surrounded by oppressive

Loneliness so loud,
Drowning out the sound
Of waves that pound at my beach.
Incessant, incessant,
Why can't you let me breathe?
Be still, sea, so that I may
Have peace!
Or be stirred, sea, that I may
Drown,
And have peace!
Or a little rest at least.
Instead you restlessly,
Oppressively, incessantly,
Surround me, lapping now
At my feet.
Let me drown,
I plead.
How selfish of me to
Wish to trap someone
On my terrible beach.
But I'm awful company
And the shellfish
Don't quite talk with me.
Yelling, no, now —scream.
But the wind that drives the waves
Carries my voice away,
Like it carried the ship away,
My weeping dissipates,
Tears lost in the ocean,
And lonely whimpers filter into the
Multitudes of sandy grains.
Until even my whisper is weak.
I'm left standing alone,
Ankle deep
In an endless, cold, black, sea
No direction,
No stars,
No landmarks,
Up is down;
Dizzy,

Stuck, and lost—
Waves, knocking at my knees.
Nowhere to wade,
No place to sleep.
No one to save,
No rescue for me.
Loneliness until I'm one
With the sea.

Rat Race

Rat cage.
Question not your purpose.
Purpose not your questions.
Simply press on, shoulder
To sweaty shoulder,
Pitter patter,
Lucky feet quickly to the finish
With gusto and heart,
Other paws drag and hurt.
Race! Race to the end,
Though the end is dirt.
If the end is out of mind,
Then the prize is in sight.
Collect your coin,
Spin again,
Take your drink,
Regret only the end.
Fight! Feel! Taste!
But do not look up
At the hand,
Lest ye be disheartened.
Lest ye forgo cheese.
Do not bite, strive for peace.
Do as all must:
Love long,
Laugh heartily,
Learn lots,
Live well.
The damned dare to
Think too much,
Look too far,
Jump too hard,
And they will fall.

Please.

The lonely mouse is heavy,
Burdened by weights about his neck

It will press.
How loud is the wordless chatter;
It's deafening, it's oppressive.
Stretch, reach for help,
Help, anyone,
Help me!
Not that they aren't willing,
But they are unable.
We're unsure if they were born
As rats,
Or if years of eyes that saw
Only straight,
And feet that ran
Side by side,
And imaginations atrophied
Incapacitated aid of any sort
To the now drowning rodent.
Alone. Yell now! Scream! SCREAM.

Please

Ye can learn, memorize,
Become happy, sad,
Mesmerised,
Feel urges, strong,
And justified.
But ye cannot understand.

Oh, to tear out my right
Eye—and give it to you
So that someone might
See the world as I do.

please

<u>Write Back!</u>

If they loved me, they'd respond;
If they liked me, they'd invite me out.
They must just want me gone.
It's because they hate me that I'm sitting,
Silent, in my house.

Just one more time-
Open that empty mailbox;
Listen again for a doorknock;
Pull your phone back out of your pocket
And hold it hoping it goes off!

Life is generally easier without me,
Nobody seeks me,
Nobody needs me,
Whenever someone is freed from my needy clinging
I hear them breathing a sigh of relief.

I'm such a nuisance,
Why do I do this?
Friendship is useless,
I'm usually so prudent,
Until in my bed, when my head hits
The pillow, got me talking stupid.

A text from hunter is spam mail,
A compliment from hunter is fan mail,
Guys think I'm too girly,
Girls think I'm a bad male.
Smothering anyone who will let me,
Until they peace out, sayonara, so long.
I am no one's favourite, if I'm out of sight,
In their minds, I'm gone.

Don't be silly, people like you plenty;
They're probably just busy, you're well-loved.
I know that, but…
why don't they respond

<u>Why I'm Lonely</u>

I'm only lonely because
My diary won't write me back, and
I'm only lonely because
My Nokia gets poor reception (when I'm about), and
I'm only lonely because
My beeper keeps running low on batts, and
I'm only lonely because
The mailman can never find my house, and
I'm only lonely because
My name has too many letters to remember
And so I never ever go out.
Wow.

These people don't get me,
But, honest, I promise
I got plenty of friends in Nebraska.
My girl's smoking hot and I visit her
In class, yeah, it's true,
She just goes to a different school,
But I'll introduce you two on the 31st of June.
You should see the way girls flirt with me
Whenever I'm not with you.
I keep getting digits, but I can only remember six.
I can tell by the way you cringe at me,
You must really want me bad.
I'm only lonely
Because my diary just won't write me back.

Nobody that knows me for very long
Likes me very much.
I sing too loud and talk too much,
Change the subject, object, and shut people down,
I can't shut up.

It must just be something about the way
My brain is wired;
I get tired of people's company,
But feel so lonely all the time.

I've tried to be myself,
And about a dozen other people,
But their personalities are all still mine.

And so I just say:
"A-Oh-Kay, uh-oh-spaghetti-O's;
Rain snow on my sunny day;
Pour Kool-Aid on my Cheerios!";
They say I'll find her one day,
But I guess I just do not know.

I have some serious suspicions of
My intentions when speaking with other humans;
Especially the women,
Because do we ever really do anything for
Someone else?

Do we ever really do anything for someone else?

Has anyone ever said or thought or done anything
That wasn't actually just for themselves?

I'll compliment you for my charisma,
I'll help you for my heart,
I'll save you for my honour,
And I'll love you forever after,
As long as you do your part.

Friends don't befriend me because
Of all their problems that they have, and
Girlfriends friend-zone me because
They're not ready for a man, and
People ignore me because
They're dumb and mean and bad. And
I'm only lonely because
My diary doesn't write me back.
I'm only lonely.

<u>Nietzsche</u>

We're all gonna die one day.
We're all gonna die one day.
We are all going to die one day.

We're all gonna cease to exist;
Return to nothingness;
Experience eternal T.V static.
Oh, we're all gonna cease to exist.

Existence is meaningless.
Life doesn't have a purpose.
We're all gonna die,
There's no how or why,
Oh, we're all gonna die one day.

Hurtling toward the void.
Hurtling toward the void.
Nothing you do matters,
But run, run, run faster.
We're hurtling toward the void.

Endless, black, abyss
Of absolute nothingness.
We are all going to die one day.

Breathing to death,
We're all dying, yet
Trying to escape the end;
Prolong our perceived experience.
Some of us are dying faster,
Some of us will die of laughter,
And some just cry 'till they're
Cross-armed in a chest.

You can't laugh when you're dead,
And you can't cry when you're dead,
You're just dead,
Naked, frozen, and tagged.

We're all just breathing to death.

We're all gonna die one day.
He said we're all gonna die one day.
Don't know where; don't care when,
But we are all going to die Some Day.

<u>A Psalm Of Death</u>

Where the sun rises for one
Comes night for another,
So as you gain some,
Drive others to hunger.

Life is fair,
For fair is it to none.
Look anywhere
And see what is done.

And from the ashes
We made more graves;
Death be not passive,
Nor be it grave,
Solely that
From which none escape.

Life is counterfeit,
Life is delusive,
And the hyphen defines its estate.
Life is nil,
Life is crude, and
The stone its final purpose.
From dust we came,
And to dust returneth,
A chapter's goal—its conclusion.

Lo, when the baby cries,
Let joy be null,
For what means life,
But another hole?

<u>Cancer Dreams</u>

It's encroaching in; you can't keep the door closed.
Hold, pull, barricade. Ok,
          The tiny thing made Its way inside—

          Tendrils burrowing until It's
In your living room.
Take out your pitchforks and torches, lasers, pills…
Make your barrages on the invasion; no stop it!

It's growing and I feel it when I sit real still,
          It aches.
Pushing on my eyes and my skull, causing a fog over
My thoughts.

          Tentacles creep and I fight, not for me,
          But for my poor family locked away safely,
          Separate from the desolation of my Enemy.
They try to help by panicking—they yell and scream
          And throw stuff at me.

I see that It will consume me,
Take me and change me,
And use me. It will chase me and safety will only
Come, for them,
          If I flee.

          So as the stench of
          Rotting seeps out from
          My nostrils,

I'll beckon my monster and leave.

<u>The Valley</u>

My friend, you see through such excited eyes—
The vast field of opportunity in life,
Taste the promise,
And pledge to frolick 'bout the flowers
Until spring's sun blinks on the valley.

Naivety takes you by the neck,
And wanton infects your spine.
You desire, yea need, to forgo the fence
And run your freedom right.

But, my friend, I'll hold you back!
Yet restrain you with fingers clinging
And forearms veiny.
For love, dear friend,
You do not know—
The bones that field has grown;
Flowers fed by human flesh,
And death, death awaiting.

<u>That's Not Me</u>

I know a light's left on for me.
I know you won't change the locks
Though you ought-
I've long lost my key.
I know your hopes when you hear a door knock,
But I promise—that's not me.

Stop sitting in the kitchen and wishing,
Stop missing,
Stop listening for my footsteps
On the porch, or a phone ring.
I know you want me home;
I know a light's left on for me;
But, I promise, I am where I ought to be.
That's not me.

<u>Do Not Cry</u>

Mother, tell me, why do you cry?
You've never given me flowers in life,
Yet you lay them now, on the earth;
Why did you rejoice my birth?

Please;
Pick up your flowers, take them home;
I cannot see them, they will not grow.
Leave, dry your tears;
They'll do nothing to prolong my years.

Stop! You're speaking to dust.
Stand we may; lie we must.
Mother, stop. You speak to dust.
Live we may; die we must.

<u>Twenty</u>

<u>Have I Loved?</u>

Have I loved?
Have I loved?
Am I capable of giving?
Or only taking? Thief I am,
I steal pride
And I gather joy,
From my hollow acts of kindness.
When those whom I call my friends die,
Most surely I will stand at their graves and cry.
And if when my children are born,
I wonder, oh how, in mystery, I wonder,
Will my tears be shed for my boy,
Or will my tears be shed for the
Wants of my own heart?
Why do we cry?
Will I love my child, will I love my wife?
Is it for joy that I mourne?

I have not loved, I have not thought,
I have not created, I have not helped,
I have not given.
I ask from Him above—
Will I ever love?

<u>The Republic Of The Gambia</u>

The consequences
Of contemplating
Such complicated
Ultimatums.
Problems came from:
Under, so fast, they are
Left, right, behind, and they even fly
Up above me.
There are starving kids living in
Gambia. Gambia?
I didn't even know Gambia
Was a country.

The Wheels On The Bus

The wheels *on the bus* go round and round,
Round and round, round and round.
These tall blue seats stare at me;
They're scaring me.
In high school, I used my words sparingly;
There's no doubt that's how I've found to
Get out of crowds.
I wasn't impoverished
Or missing a father to parent me;
In my school, I was just a typical kid,
At least apparently.

And furthermore, I swear that we
As Christians habitually forget
Our great given commission,
Of which Matthew 28 will speak,
And we so easily miss what it means
To repent from sin and listen to Jesus' teachings;
And then share what we read through preaching
To the unbelieving, so that
They might be with us in eternity.
We won't share our gift of which we are unworthy,
Because on Earth, we know that if we stand out,
Then we don't fit in, and
When fitting in is your existence,
That's a scary thing.

So, in silence, I sit. I'm a quiet kid,
I'm just hiding my eyes from all of life's violence.
My hoodie would keep my head down,
And my walkman protects my ears
From the most vile of kids.

But, then… Her name was Abby;
A flower; a peony, or rose,
And she acted so much happier
Than any of you could possibly know.
She was actually beautiful,

With her kindness,
She would stand out from other kids.
She was so loved.

And she had a nice little necklace about her neck
With an inscription that simply read, "*why*"
And so I would poke fun and ask, "*Why* what?"
And she would just smile and shrug.
I loved that nice little necklace so much
Because "*why*" was something
I knew nothing about, but Abby,
Abby had it all figured out.

I was wrong, Abby's smile brought me so much light,
But there was something going on;
Not something in her life, outside, it was alright,
But travesty was happening inside of Abby's mind;
She was dying.

Abby's throat was sore from choking on
All those questions her neck kept asking;
Answers lying past her pendant;
She'd lose her independence
To that inquisitive sentence
That pressed upon her esophagus incessantly;
Strangled, death penalty penance…
Till she was only able to gasp and ask *why*
A noose she's tying?
Why are we here? And *why* is she so used to crying?

I never saw past her big blue eyes.
She desired to be euthanized.
I promised myself that I'd ask Abby to my church,
Eventually,
But now I probably never will,
Because even though she was surrounded by friends,
She felt hollow still. And so one weekend,
Drunk and alone, Abby grabbed a bottle
And happened to swallow a handful of pills.
340 mg of oxycodone,

That lethal dose slid down her throat and
Ran right past her nice little necklace that
Finally, let her lie still.

Abby left me her nice little necklace in her
Nice little will.
And to this day, every day,
Whenever I pray, I'm asking God, *"why"* still.
I think He just smiles and shrugs,
Because I loved Abby,
I just didn't love her enough.
Why, still. *Why*. Still.

Still, *the wheels on the bus* go round and round,
Round and round, round and round;
Rolling along like someone dropped an Advil
And those tall blue seats, like Ibuprofen,
Still stare at me;
And I've been hoping that they'll stop scaring me,
But still, I swear I'll keep backing down and down.

Why do I refuse to give forgiveness;
Haven't I been forgiven most?
Why do I refuse to cry and love,
In what, possibly, have I to boast?

The ambassador of light hides in darkness,
The harbinger of love does naught but loathe,
I ignored Abby's heart because I was heartless,
I stayed far enough apart for her to stay alone.

She closed her eyes thinking she was worthless,
She fell asleep feeling unloved,
She clung to some seed of hatred sown by Satan
In her youth.
And I guess I never let her know the truth.
I, the watchman, let my guard down,
And let a lie infect her,
She believed that life was meaningless,
And I never bothered to correct her.

She asked me if I believed in Jesus,
And I said that I didn't.
She begged me to tell her of Heaven,
But we couldn't witness.
She asked me to pray for her, but I never did.
I've done a lot of praying ever since.

She didn't ask with her words,
Her mouth was too filled with assurances,
But by her broken smile and broken eyes, I could tell.

Listen again, it gets worse. I said
They don't always ask with their words;
Their mouths had cages as if braces made a cell.
But, as clear as ice, I could always tell.

They're simply defending themselves,
Seeking peace in violent acts;
And Abby, so tired of preceding *Z's*,
Just needed to take a nice little nap;
Well, I guess she woke up somewhere else;
Now I find my conscience constantly
With my lost friends in Hell.

<u>Tell Me How To Live</u>

Tell me how to live;
Tell me where happiness is;
Tell me what is love and what isn't;
Tell me of the subtleties of life;
Tell me of strength and of weakness;
Tell me the truth in all the lies;
Tell me the truth and nothing less.

I look at the kid I've never seen,
And I see him;
He too once had dreams,
But now he's done dreaming.

And that girl's mom just got diagnosed;
And she asked me "why her"
She was good; so, why was it so?
She asked me why good people hurt.
Please tell me, because I do not know.

Watch a movie and you'll see
The main hero saving everything;
And every single human being,
Ever, always, will always think
That, "That person up there is me!"
But much more realistically,
We're the person walking past, in the back
Of the screen, that nobody ever sees;
Hardly scripted, because we are
Inconsequential blips in
The cosmic scheme of things.
Sonder.

I'm the person who adds a past tense
To the word dreams.
Dreamt.
Tell me please, because I'm not stressed;
I'm just equally bored of everything.

Tell me, please—what to take,
And what to give,
And who to hate,
And who to kiss.
You don't have to tell me
What in the heck is this,
But please, please, just tell me
How to live.

Nothing Special

I'm just like everyone else, I guess.
I'm nothing special. I have the same emotions—
I just cope with them in a broken way.
Somewhere in my brain I might be special,
But it's our actions that define us,
And on a page, our resumes are all the same.

<u>Blacksmith</u>

I am a blacksmith.
'Tis metal that I work with
And it's with violence
That I strike iron,
I beat ingots with vengeance,
With my lies I stoke fire,
Hatred is the billow of my furnace,
Lust is the flux
I dunk my piece in
An attempt to prevent rust,
But the corrosive nature
Of the wicked fuller
That metal is touched with;
Slag, cracks, and chips will win.

I create three single pieces;
Three works of my hands.
My anvil of pride
And my hammer of fear.
I am a man;
And I forge with my sin—
Simply three little nails,
What terrible things,
These three nails forged by me—
Two for His hands and one for His feet.

<u>Romans 7</u>

That which I desire eludes my grasp.
That which I hate seems to be prowling
Like a lion at my path.

What I do not want—that I do.
What I want—that I do not do.
God gave me freedom, slack on my leash
To prove my worth and I ~~failed~~ fail miserably;
Choking myself as I chase that golden calf that
Satan dangles in my view;
Idolic statues that I choose.

It's all naught in light of God;
Nothing stands next to Him.
Curse my nearsightedness,
This blindness pride has wrought.
Curse my curse of sin, crouching at my door.
When He holds out his nail-riven hands,
I'll wish I had given Him more.

But, because of Jesus, bless His Name:
I, without worth, am free.
0 days since my last mistake;
0 days since He's forgiven me.
He bore my shameful deeds,
Claimed God's wrath in full,
Now I stand redeemed. A righteous, blameless soul.

<u>Ferocious Grace</u>

God, have I studied
The universe your word holds together?
Under the weight of your awesome works
I've often cried;
And bound in humbling
Mystery I am to wonder:
What am I, O God, what am I—
That you should have a heart for mine?

Could I outrun your mercies—
I would have.
Father you know
I've often tried.

Bought with blood; you have granted me salvation!
A slave no more, now free.
Who stands to accuse? Not even Satan!
Sin, shame, and death can but claw at my feet.

I were a wretched man a-running
Swift away from thee;
Chasing idols of destruction,
Until your Grace, with such ferocity,
Sought and tackled me.

In heaven, my deeds will show as nothing:
All as loss, all as loss.
So I succumb to shame.
Then when my crimes are read;
Sins laid bare I'm blamed—
I'll point to the cross, to the cross.
The interceder has wiped all charges clean.

And ne'er the likes a pardon been.

<u>On My Way</u>

I don't know where I'm going,
My destination is unknown, and
I guess that I'm still hoping,
To fix what is so broken.
I look around my house,
And my street,
My school,
And my town,
And at me,
And I know that this place is not my home.
I am not home;
This is not where I belong.
So sick of not going anywhere,
This road will take me home,
On this highway, wind in my hair,
Which one it is, I do not know,

But if you have no destination—
Any road will take you there.

I'm running there so fast,
So eager to arrive,
And all these people pass,
Happy to just survive.
I cannot take it anymore.
Everything always the same,
Some people run in circles,
But in their place, they'll stay.
I have no idea where I'm going—
But I know I'm on my way.

<u>Wow, how lost I am.</u>

         Wow, how lost I am.
I've found
That to not look about, out
At the planet around
Is to dispel awe in the eye.
Mountains lick the sky
Like the tongue of a mouth.
Oh; what of the clouds?
How Earth spins about her axis
And Coriolis will act as this planet's
Lungs as it exhales an endless
Breath from above;
Blowing a wee kiss of love
To the trees down under
Which creak and shudder as winds will howl.
…
         I have hands
Ten digits and a match
With a boxed in striker.
Just a phosphorus stick with which
My fingers will pick
A long, thin, lighter.
And though my bones squeak, groan, growl,
My hands and fingertips grip the Bic to strike
And invoke Oppenheimer
I blow the light to life, forming smoke,
Stoking fire.
…
         My mind
Will write faster than my hand, and in life—
Thinking twelve steps ahead
      Leaves you two steps behind.

<u>Tiny Dining Table</u>

The tragedy of a tiny dining table
In a large kitchen:
A lonely mansion and breakfasts eaten separately.
Oh, the woes of single-serve T.V. dinners
Stacked in an extra-large fridge.
How sad, the empty echoes
Of a large suburban house
With separate screens for every bedroom,
And no welcome mat.
The tragedy of a tiny dining table.

And the joy of folding lawn chairs,
Set out in the weeds.
Laughter of an open door and
Piles of shoes on the porch.
Dinner trays set to sofas,
A fireplace and a backyard.
The wonder in the eyes of children
Sat down on a tailgate with a cold hot dog.
The tragedy of a tiny dining table,
And, oh, the joy of folding lawn chairs.

<u>Communication</u>

I can wiggle my tongue and blow
    And make you think my thoughts.

I can scratch a pen on paper
    And make you feel my feelings.

I can hit a rock with a chisel,
    And 8,000 years from now,
    Some scholar may know my knowledge.

    Maybe, if I'm prolific,
Some poor student will be forced to read it
For an English project.
    After I'm long dead.

I can strike a keyboard
    And cause a stranger
    To cry my tears.

See that you have a story,
    Now assemble words to share it.

<u>Not</u>

If only there was *no* word—
To describe what *isn't*.
Oh what a blessing;
If *empty* was *emptied*
From our dictionaries;
If *bare* was *barely* used;
Scarce, *scarcely* spewed;
Nothing *never* muttered.
Oh, to bury *hole* in a cemetery.
Screw the *void*; fill back the *gap*;
Can the *nary*.
Because, language, for centuries,
Has been *lacking whole*;
And instead, we see the cup
Always as half *empty*
And *never* as half *full*.

<u>Mother Of Mine</u>

How can I say thank you to the girl
Who literally gave me this world
But would never give me up to this world
She raised me and still
She's amazing for real
She's great she
Literally made me
How can I give thanks
In a way that says I recognize that
You've sacrificed much
And for that I am grateful
You packed me my lunch
Man what an angel

She birthed me and my brothers
I'm undeserving of such a mother
She's worth all the love her
Turds of kids can muster

I cry when she cries,
And my momma cry cuz of my pain;
I know sometimes it seems like
The world leans till your spine breaks,
But I'll be on your side,
And if anyone looks at you sideways—
I'll rip their head off their neck
So I can stick it back on the right way.
All I'm saying
Is—Thank you for all that you do.
You've dried tears when kids cried,
Kissed and applied bandaids,
Sent backhands when I bad-mouthed,
Gave comfort on my bad days.
My mom is an angel,
Thank God for her, I pray
I live long enough
To pay back all the love my mom gave.

<u>Can Of Beans</u>

Should e're a lone creek, cold
Run through your bare toes—

And if you should find old oaks
To be a ceiling o'er your lost head—

Should a sharp rock pierce the sole of your heel
And draw blood into the river to whisper downstream
Over softer stones that make up footprints—

If branches establish the walls of your house—

If headlights of cars cast jagged shadows to flicker
Across your face from a lone stretch of Interstate,
A wooded run away—

If cell service bars are found only
On top of the hill,
You dare not turn on your phone from
Under your lean-to tarp,
Because you haven't any abundance of charge—

Should a can of beans heated by a
Small, burning pile of
Garbage and twigs become your only friend—

Talk to yourself, keep on walking,
Enjoy the feel of the earth on your feet,
The warm trash on your face,
And be content.

<u>Sleep On Couches</u>

Sleep on couches,
Shower with travel sized hotel soap,
Drink from a styrofoam cup,
Take calls on a track phone,
Don't get too cozy;
You're not home.

Sleep on couches,
Shower with travel sized hotel soap,
Drink from a styrofoam cup,

<u>The Chair</u>

There is sand that longs to
        Tickle your toes;

Waves which desire to
        Lick your skin;

Brush that yearns to
        Play with your clothes;

While mountains crave the
        Taste of your sweat;

It's the flowers' wish to
        Kiss your nose;

Somewhere wind needs to
        Ruffle your hair;

And branches want to
        Hold your hand;

Life yet to be lived,
        The world out there—
So put down this book,
        And go love your planet.

<u>Bring Me The Horizon</u>

Bring me the heavens,
Bring me the depths,
Set me free to roam,
Just please, please,
Don't let me, not once again,
Rest my head on a bed I know.

Set the sails,
Spur the mount,
Loose the cords of Orion.
Be it distant planets, foreign nations,
Or desert islands;
I care not the means or mode-
Just bring me that horizon!

<u>Mitochondria, The Cosmos, And Cruise Control</u>

You know what it feels like to
Sit tight at midnight on a still highway.
As yellow grass and hills
And the occasional road sign float by.
You know hands that grip
A stationary steering wheel so light,
And the sound of wind against
Your imperceptible motion.
You know snow
That sends your vehicle into warp drive,
Icy stars that avoid your cockpit
As the black unknown races past.
You know of bassy static crackle that
Pours from a stereo and rumbles
Through your head and fills your ear canals,
Pressing on your temples.
Cut your brights.

You know what it feels like to
Harness the awesome power
Of organic matter,
Long dead, baked and compressed.
A thousand horses under your feet
Scream as Boyle is invoked
And explosions steam,

And yet you also know what it feels like
To yawn and want sleep.
You know of other headlights
Seen through heavy eyelids.
Flashing you awake
And causing you to tap gently
On your brakes and
Feel, finally, acceleration.

You know of
Musty carpet, mustard coloured, worn, and
Well read, near memorised.

You know of water-stained
Ceiling panels
And the electric whirr of
Fluorescent lights,
Industrial hum of air vents,
And the hiss of hot water pipes.
You know endless empty hallways walked
A thousand times.

You know the perfect song of a mighty humpback
Ringing throughout the deep,
And the call of a great sea giant
Reaching to the base of the mountains.
Black trenches that stretch to the crushing depths
Commanded by an eerie
And omnipresent strain
Sung by a lonely whale,
Longing for a kindly ear.

You know a fourth a tank of gasoline
And heater that works behind
A quarter-inch of glass to keep
The frozen air at bay.
That gas and that fan and that glass
Are all that stands between
Yourself and death.
Millimetres of windowpane
Support the full weight
Of your fragile life.
Maybe you'd survive 3 hours
If you huddled up and held your breath.

You know loud, echoing, clicking steps
Of heels, bearing a slightly
Overweight, nice enough,
Bored, middle-aged lady with
Glasses and a sarcastic quote printed out and
Scotch-taped to
Her regretful metal desk.

You know the busy bustle of
Rush hour, car horns sound sporadically
Like popcorn in a microwave,
Suits that walk with a purpose,
You know shoulder bumps
And quick time march.
Eyes down, chin tucked,
Get to work, go to lunch,
Back to work, run.
You know the buzz, the all
Important continuous buzz
That never stops, until,
Until it's time to learn to knit,
Shop for coffins.

You know the roar of a star,
Of our sun, as she rages and burns;
Hurling destruction
And chaos out into nothing.
Perpetually unleashing her wrath,
The raw and unfathomable
Power of a million flaming whips
Lashing out into the abyss
Catching the glimmer of a satellite,
Too small not to miss,
As it drifts by at a cool
.0001% lightspeed.
You know our home planet
Hurtling through
The vacuum, clinging on to
Thin, invisible strings of gravity.
You know how a mere eight-and-a-half
Minutes away is this ball
Of instant death, too large
And scary to comprehend.
You know what the sun feels like,
Our oasis in the nothing, our single candle flame
Floating alone in the endless empty black,
Bobbing along in the open galactic ocean:
Our warmth, our light and our life.

Do not look directly at it.

You know of a worn couch,
Fabricated in an older generation,
Patched partially with duct tape,
Claiming for itself a distinct squeak
When your blue jeans meet upholstery.
You know of no comparably
Uncomfortable amount of give
In a seat.
The smell of a thousand butts
And the trapped soul of a thousand farts.
Food stains from the '70s.
Crumbs and quarters found
In between the cushions keep things interesting.
You know
The carpenter that crafted this sofa looks
Down at you from heaven with pity
As your mind wanders.
Sitting and pretending to listen
To someone you don't care to hear speak.

You know the excruciating agony
Of a yawn interrupted
Before its climax that ends in
A disappointing empty breath.
An incessant itch in your soul
That you cannot scratch.
Pain matched only by a blinding
Migraine or femur cracked in half.

You know a restless and agnostic head
Set upon a pillow, and thoughts that press,
Questions that burrow and you know the feeling
Of being hit by the train. You know the weight
Of remembering
How mysteriously numbered are your days.
You know nothing other than the absence of light;
The endless black night
That compresses and constricts your conscience.

And floods your nostrils.
You know not, nor could you comprehend the totality
Of the insignificance that you feel now only a sliver,
A fraction,
Of the endless absolute.

You know the miracle of childbirth
The love in a mother's eye
And the first cry of a baby
With an entire life ahead of him
To live, mistakes to be made
So much to learn, so much to take,
So much to give.
Chromosomes woven with care,
Frail bones pieced together,
Wrapped with tendons and tissues,
Packaged so neat, and so cute,
And so temporary, and so…
Useless.
You know a future, a past,
Hardships and breathtaking beauty.
You know truth, and life.

You know the loneliness
Of a Sunday evening
Of a wasted day, of
Hours spent doing little more than
Breathing,
You know the melancholic ache
Of waking only to return to sleeping.

You know the peace
Of a green hill, under a
Golden autumn tree,
Warmed by morning's sun floating slowly above.
Dying flowers twitch as
An invisible breeze plucks
The strings of a hundred-acre cello.
You know the freedom
Of a leaf released from

Branches and let loose
To dance down the street,
Now reflectively wet with light raindrop kisses,
Gifts from the clouds
That watch over the humanoid patch
Of matted grass that your back
Left in the growing shadow of the oak.

You know wild raspberries.
You know a silent drive alone.
You know the restless
Mitochondria of the red blood cell.
You know that couch.
You know.

I know nothing,
But I feel a little.

<u>Dear Danger,</u>

Against a spray of stinging salt;
Against wind, wave, and thunder flash;
Against a wall of nature's wrath;
I cling for life to my dear mast,
And in the face of certain death—
I rear my head to laugh.

In the cold, against the snow,
And pain that numbs my toes.
In the drought of desert heat,
Or black of caves, wet and deep,
Still, I hunt all threats of Death,
And still my hunger screams.

Come now, Danger, know my name;
Hurl at me all you have saved.
Come now, Danger, don't leave me bored.
I'll not go 'till I'm satisfied,
And I, dear Danger, yearn for more.

Angry, now, Danger deals me lash on lash,
In vain hopes to see me wince,
But when Danger comes for me again—
He'll find only my unbroken grin.

A little rain shan't shake my faith,
And pain is only pain.
Come now, Danger, you've exhausted all;
And still, I'm truly unafraid.

As my vessel creaks and yaws,
Feels stress's sting so sharp,
Still, I'll stare down Death's dull jaws,
Onwards, until dawn, I'll march.

Another dawn, or final set,
Is not for me to pick;
And, earnestly, I'll call your bet;

I'm impartial as to which.

If senility finds me, or in my youth,
Is not for me to choose,
But you, Danger, can take not from me—
There's naught I stand to lose.

Even should Satan come
To drag me to the depths,
Still, you have no power over me;
I'll rage on to Death.

Come now, danger, know your place.
You will show respect.

For, you, my dear friend danger,
No more a stranger be,
You, my dear friend danger, address
A man, content and free.

So you may suck my carcass into that black abyss;
Swallow my beloved ship in whole,
But, because I will stand in Faith of this:
You, dear danger, can't touch my soul.

<u>God, Break My Heart</u>

God, break my heart;
Bring me to my knees;
Take me apart,
And reform me
The way you want me to be.

God, give me tears;
God, let me weep;
God, lay me low;
God, make me weak.

God, break my heart,
And let me sing.
God, bring me close,
And hasten to complete
Your perfect work in me.

<u>If Rocks Could Talk</u>

If the seas could speak, she'd say
How the ocean was spoken into being
On the first day, the swells would tell
Of how the Spirit moved and Ghost dwelt;
Waves would recall words uttered from
The lips of God that parted waters
And left sea sand and rocks parched
To be filled with grass and birds
And living, breathing art.
With fish that swam at his command
And brilliant lights that shine from
Billions of satellites and stars,
Gas giants, Mars, and black holes.
Until from dust, His words wrote: "Man."
Braiding his X and Y chromosomes,
Breathing life into his bones.

If rocks could talk they'd tell
Of when a wicked serpent curled his tail,
Wrapped up in branches of trees,
Raveling, weaving,
Planting his seed;
He shambled through leaves
And handed to Eve
An apple to eat.
With the world's first question ever asked,
Hissed out, as a snake's split tongue
Flicked and spat just a lick of doubt
Into humanity's heart.
Rocks undoubtedly watched
As teeth of calcium split and parted
The skin of a fig;
Or maybe innocence fled lips
That pecked and kissed a pear.
There the rocks saw
How Woman had bitten into
The forbidden fruit
And Man followed suit.

Pebbles quivered and stones shivered
As God introduced thorns and blood
And Man began his destruction.
The mountains gazed upon Abraham
As he led his beloved son up one of them
To raise a blade to plunge,
To gut him open,
Then God spoke a "stop"
And the rocks along with the ocean,
Relieved, released the breath they'd been holding.

If trees could speak they'd breathe
The story of how after Eve was born The offspring
And through the shaming and pain
Of our Saviour came redeeming glory.
They would elaborate
On pierced hands, steel driven and whip stricken,
Mallets that hammered and hit,
Splinters dig as scoffers spit.
The branches He carried
Could recreate breaths drawn in pain
As tendons ripped and rib cages caved,
And when the debt of man's sin He payed,
Rebellion forgave,
The lips of God spake:
"It is finished."

The ocean, the mountains, and the leaves
Knew the purpose of their existence
When darkness was expelled by the Word of Light
And death had lost its sting
The sea, the rocks, and the trees
Were joined by humanity,
His praise to sing for eternity.

<u>Ashes</u>

As I came into this world, so shall I leave,
Naked and bare and with nothing.
As but a vapour, I'll live Love,
With every breath You put in my lungs
Until I return to dust.

<u>Floating</u>

Sweet dreams—
Ocean, star speckled-sky,
Bright with a million pinholes,
Peppered by.
You slow your breath, floating on
Placid water, black with night.
The horizon is disappeared,
And there exists no line
Between reflected stars that your
Fingers can reach,
And the twinkles of suns
Among other galaxies above.
Touch one—and
The slightest movement
Sends out ripples which disrupt the heavens—
Goodnight.

I Took A Shower With My Socks On.

squish squish

Fin.